NIGERIA

LORNA ROBSON

Facts On File, Inc.

Nigeria

Copyright © 2005 by Evans Brothers, Limited

Facts On File, Inc.
132 West 31st Street
New York NY 10001

Library of Congress Cataloging-in-Publication Data

Robson, Lorna, 1970–
  Nigeria / Lorna Robson.
    p. cm. — (Countries of the world)
  Includes index.
  ISBN 0-8160-6010-X
  1. Nigeria—Juvenile literature. I. Title. II. Countries of
the world (Facts On File, Inc.)
  DT515.22.R63 2005
  966.9—dc22
                2005040689

Facts On File books are available at special discounts
when purchased in bulk quantities for businesses,
associations, institutions, or sales promotions. Please
call our Special Sales Department in New York at
(212) 967-8800 or (800) 322-8755.

You can find Facts On File on the World Wide Web at
http://www.factsonfile.com.

Printed in China by Leo Paper Products Ltd.

10 9 8 7 6 5 4 3 2 1

Editor: Susie Brooks
Designer: Mayer Media, Ltd.
Map artwork: Peter Bull
Charts and graphs: Encompass Graphics, Ltd.

Photograph acknowledgments
All by Lorena Ros/Easi-Images and Roy Maconachie/
Easi-Images except: 19, 29 top, 35 (Eric Miller, Link
Picture Library/iAfrika Photos); 29 bottom (Reuters/STR).

First published by Evans Brothers Limited,
2A Portman Mansions, Chiltern Street, London
W1U 6NR, United Kingdom.

This edition published under license from Evans Brothers
Limited. All rights reserved.

Endpapers (front): The streets of Lagos bustle
with people and cars at all hours of the day.
Title page: Markets, such as this one in Benin
City, serve as important arenas for business
and trade.
Imprint and Contents pages: In Nigeria's
delta region, giant oil tankers can be found
alongside traditional fishing boats.
Endpapers (back): One of the old slave ports
near Badagri, from which thousands of slaves
were shipped to plantations in the Caribbean
and the Americas beginning in the 1500s.

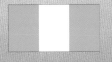

The Nigerian flag consists of two vertical bands
of green, representing agriculture, and one
band of white, signifying unity and peace.

Lagos is the most populous city in Nigeria and the African continent.

Modern Nigeria is "big" in many different ways. It is one of the largest countries in West Africa. It has the greatest population of any African country – one in seven Africans is a Nigerian. It is the main producer of oil in Africa and is an important contributor to the continent as a whole.

A COUNTRY OF CONTRASTS

Nigeria is a country of contrasts. Many people are desperately poor, but a very few – mainly city dwellers – are extremely rich. The country has an array of beautiful, open landscapes, as well as huge cities that are as chaotic, polluted and crowded as any in the world.

Nigeria has numerous ethnic and religious groups who speak many different languages. Before European conquest in the nineteenth century, the country was home to an estimated 250 ethnic groups who traded and lived among each other for centuries but were each governed separately. Since independence in 1960, Nigeria has been a federal republic, which is now divided into 36 states and one federal territory.

ONE LAND, MANY HISTORIES

Nearly all the ethnic groups of Africa are represented in Nigeria, so the country's history is really a patchwork of these different peoples' pasts. Some of the earliest known settlers were the Nok people of the Jos Plateau in central Nigeria. They established an advanced civilization around 500 B.C., and their tradition for arts and crafts continues today.

From around A.D. 500, the Hausa and Fulani peoples of northern Nigeria developed strong trading links with North Africa across the Sahara Desert. The Islamic religion was soon introduced along these routes. At the same time, the southwest was dominated by the Yoruba empires, while in the east the Kingdom of Benin developed (not to be confused with modern-day Benin), and in the southeast the Igbos established their diverse culture.

EUROPEAN IMPACT

The Yoruba kingdoms were the first to make contact with early Portuguese spice traders in the fifteenth century. Then Britain became involved, trading in other commodities such as palm oil, peanuts, and even slaves. The north remained largely unaffected by contact with the Europeans until the nineteenth century.

NIGERIA'S STATES

By this time, missionaries had brought Christianity to the south, which began to conflict with the spread of Islam in the north. Religion is still the cause of much unrest in Nigeria today.

In 1861 Nigeria was made a British colony, and by 1914 the country that is now Nigeria was all a British colony. British rule remained until 1960, when Nigeria became a republic as part of a wave of African countries declaring independence.

THE BIAFRA WAR

From the outset of independence there was a power struggle among the different ethnic groups. It seemed that as soon as one government took control, an opposing ethnic group would take over in a coup d'etat. In 1967 the Igbos attempted to break away from the rest of Nigeria and declared the Republic of Biafra. This led to one of the most brutal civil wars of the twentieth century. It lasted for three years, by the end of which at least 100,00 soldiers were killed and up to 2 million civilians died of starvation.

MODERN-DAY NIGERIA

In the late 1950s, oil was discovered in commercial quantities in Nigeria. People thought the nation would become rich, but – for a variety of different reasons that will be explained in this book – this did not happen. Nigeria today is struggling to pick up the pieces after decades of military dictatorships, characterized by human rights abuses and repression. The country finally returned to civilian rule and democracy in 1999 under the leadership of President Olusegun Obasanjo.

Nigeria's youthful population is increasing rapidly and is likely to continue to do so in the near future.

KEY DATA

Official Name:	Federal Republic of Nigeria
Area:	923,770km^2
Population:	137,250,000 (2004 estimate)
Official Language:	English
Capital City:	Abuja
Other Main Cities:	Lagos, Kano, Benin City, Ibadan
GDP Per Capita:	US$860*
Currency:	naira (NGN)
Exchange Rate:	US$1 = 129.51 naira £1 = 243.94 naira

*(2002) Calculated on Purchasing Power Parity basis. Sources: World Bank; UN

LANDSCAPE AND CLIMATE

Mangrove swamps line the south coast and provide a unique ecosystem for birds and fish.

Nigeria is generally a fairly flat country, but it has a wide range of different landscapes. These include dry semideserts, open grasslands and hills, mountainous areas, tropical rain forests and mangrove swamps.

LAND USE

About 40 percent of Nigeria's land surface is used for intensive crop agriculture. Pasture for grazing animals, such as cattle and goats, takes up another 20 percent, while just over 6 percent is forests and woodlands. Two major rivers flow through Nigeria – the Niger and the Benue.

ROCKS AND SOILS

The land and soils of much of north and southwest Nigeria are formed from crystalline igneous (volcanic) rocks which are part of the African Shield. This is an ancient layer of very hard rocks that are resistant to erosion, so the plateaus and hills here are quite high. The rocks are

LANDSCAPE FEATURES

NIGER

CHA

SOKOTO BASIN

Sokoto

Lake Chad

CHAD BASIN

Kano

Kainji Reservoir

Kaduna

JOS PLATEAU

BENIN

Kainji Dam

Abuja

Benue

EASTERN HIGHLANDS

Dimlang 2,042m

CAMEROON

COASTAL LOWLANDS

Lagos

Bight of Benin

Niger

Chappal Waddi 2,419m

Gulf of Guinea

Niger Delta

Bight of Biafra

0   300km

0   200 miles

Nigeria's remaining tropical rain forests are a rich resource, but they are threatened by human use in some regions.

level. Lagos – the largest city in sub-Saharan Africa – is built on an island created by West Africa's biggest lagoon. Harbors are scattered nearby, but these need constant dredging because sand levels are high. This is due to the Guinea Current, which moves material along the coast.

HILLS, PLAINS AND PLATEAUS

Stretching inland from the coast is an area of low, gently undulating plains and scattered hills, covered in thick tropical rain forest. This extends for about 250km, then continues up into the basins of the Niger and Benue Rivers.

rich in minerals, providing Nigeria with some valuable natural resources. The soils tend to be fertile, though in the north this is not always the case.

In the southeast and in the low-lying northeast and northwest corners of the country – the Chad and Sokoto Basins – the land is made up of younger sedimentary rocks. These form light, sandy soils but they are less fertile and less resistant to erosion than the older rocks.

LANDSCAPES OF THE SOUTH

Southern Nigeria borders the Atlantic Ocean. The coastline extends for 800km and consists mainly of low sedimentary plains.

THE NIGER DELTA

The delta of the Niger River juts into the Gulf of Guinea in the eastern Atlantic. It is one of the largest river deltas in the world and is Nigeria's main oil-producing region. The delta covers a huge area and is an intricate network of streams, mangrove swamps, islands, lagoons and sand bars.

THE COASTAL LOWLANDS

To the east and west of the delta are the coastal lowlands – areas of sandy beaches, indented by numerous palm-fringed lagoons and creeks. These lowlands rarely rise over 30m above sea

LOCATING NIGERIA

Nigeria lies north of the equator between 4° and 14° north latitude and between 3° and 15° east longitude. It measures 1,200km from east to west and 1,050km from north to south at its widest points. It is bordered by Benin to the west, Niger to the north, Chad to the northeast and Cameroon to the east. To the south is the Atlantic Ocean.

Nigeria's coastal waters provide local fishers with an important livelihood, here near Badagri.

INLAND LANDSCAPES

Inland from the coastal region, the land rises to escarpments (cliffs or steep slopes of rock). These form the rocky terrain of the central plateaus. To the east are Nigeria's mountains, while in the far northeast and northwest the landscape is low and flat.

THE EASTERN HIGHLANDS

The Eastern Highlands are the only mountains in Nigeria. They lie along the border with Cameroon and are made up of several separate ranges and plateaus. In the Shebeshi Mountains is Nigeria's highest point – Dimlang (2,042m) – sometimes known as Vogel Peak. Also in this area are crater lakes with warm thermal springs, created by ancient volcanoes. Many swift-flowing rivers have their source in these mountains and flow into the Benue River. The area is sparsely populated.

THE CENTRAL AND NORTHERN PLATEAUS

North of the valleys of the Niger and the Benue, and around the center of the country, lies a fairly flat plateau area. The average height above sea level is about 700m. Rivers have cut into the plateau, eroding the rock. The vegetation is open grassland – known as savannah – which is occasionally interrupted by outcropping granite hills called inselbergs. This is Nigeria's main agricultural area and it is heavily populated.

The vegetation becomes sparser, with fewer trees and shrubs, and the climate drier toward the north. The land extends through a relatively fertile region, where Nigeria's main grazing is found, to a dry expanse in the extreme north. This is known as the Sahelian zone and is basically an area of semidesert.

THE CHAD AND SOKOTO BASINS

The northeastern and northwestern tips of Nigeria form the Chad and Sokoto Basins. Here, the land drops to below 300m, forming depressions into which rivers drain. The Sokoto River and its tributaries flow through the Sokoto Basin and deposit large quantities of sediment to create broad floodplains. This area is also highly

Yankari National Park is an important wildlife sanctuary, but it is also known for its hot springs.

CASE STUDY
THE JOS PLATEAU

Jos has a temperate climate because of its elevation, and it is well suited for dairy farming and vegetable production.

The Jos Plateau is a relatively high area of granite and volcanic rocks. It covers an area of about 8,000km^2, rising out of the middle of Nigeria and forming the largest landmass over 1,000m. With its rugged · terrain of volcanic plugs jutting out of wide savannah grasslands, the plateau boasts some spectacular scenery. On the southwest slopes, heavy rainfall feeds small patches of rain forest.

The plateau forms a watershed from which streams flow to Lake Chad in the north and to the rivers Niger and Benue in the south. The higher altitudes and cooler temperatures combine to draw rainfall from passing clouds. Because of its pleasant climate and the fact that it is freer from diseases than the surrounding lowlands, this region has one of the highest population densities in the country. During the colonial era this is where many Europeans liked to live. The rich soils and favorable climate provided an excellent environment for growing European vegetables, such as potatoes, and also for a dairy industry.

The town of Jos (with a population of 510,300) is the major settlement on the plateau, despite the fact that Nigeria's capital Abuja (population 107,069) is also located here. Jos is considered by many to be Nigeria's most attractive city. It grew up around tin mines at the beginning of the twentieth century. Tin is still mined and processed in this area, although the industry has declined in recent years because aluminum is now more widely used.

influenced by wind action and is often covered by drifting sands. Both basins are intensively cultivated with the help of irrigation. Low-lying wetland areas, or *fadamas* (see page 21), are particularly important sites for agriculture. Artesian reservoirs – aquifers of water stored below the ground – are another useful source of water here.

Zuma Rock, a famous granite outcrop, marks the edge of Abuja.

CLIMATE

Nigeria's climate is hot all year round, with distinctive rainy seasons. The country lies entirely within the Tropics, yet there are wide climatic variations. The main difference between the north and the south of the county is the much higher rainfall and humidity nearer the coast. In addition, the higher land of the Jos Plateau and the Eastern Highlands tends to be cooler than elsewhere.

NIGERIA'S SEASONS

In Nigeria it is more common to talk about rainy and dry seasons than summer and winter. Nigerian seasons are controlled by the movement of two air masses – warm, moist air from the Atlantic and hot, dry air from the Sahara Desert. The area where they meet is called the intertropical convergence zone. During the summer months of April to September this zone moves slowly northward, bringing most of the country under the influence of moisture-laden maritime air. This is when Nigeria experiences its rainy season. Then the zone moves south, leaving the north exposed to the hot, dry, Saharan air mass again.

THE VARIABLE NORTH

The rainy season in the north lasts from late May to the end of September. The Hausa people divide the seasons into four main catagories – the dry, cool season *(kaka)*, the dry, hot season *(bazara),* the wet, warm season *(damina)* and the dry, warm season *(rani).*

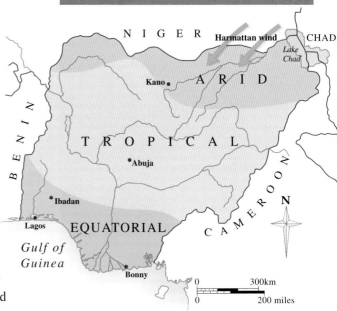

CLIMATE ZONES

The beaches and sunshine of the south coast, here on the Lekki Peninsula, are popular for day trips.

Leading up to the rainy season, between March and May, temperatures can reach as high as 45°C, or 113°F. They can fall as low as 6°C (43°F) at night during December and January. The average rainfall in the north is 500–750mm. However, for at least five months of the year there is no rainfall at all and the area sometimes suffers from droughts. Droughts have become more frequent in recent years, and experts say the last 100 years have been among the driest for several centuries. Droughts in the 1970s and 1980s severely affected large areas of northern Nigeria; crops failed, cattle died and, in some cases, people died too. It is possible that these droughts are part of a much larger change in the world's climate as a whole.

THE EQUATORIAL SOUTH

The climate in the south can be described as equatorial. This means it is generally hot and wet for most of the year. It is strongly affected by the moist air mass that moves northward from the Atlantic Ocean.

The most rainfall comes between April and July and in September and October, and it can be extremely heavy. Bonny, a town on the southeast coast, has an average rainfall of more

The equatorial south receives heavy rainfall, especially during September and October.

than 4,000mm per year. This is five times the annual rainfall of Minneapolis, Minnesota. People are advised to keep water channels and drains clear in order to avoid flooding, which is a common problem. Although the temperatures here are, on average, slightly cooler than in the north, the high humidity makes it feel much hotter and more uncomfortable.

CASE STUDY
THE HARMATTAN WIND

The Harmattan is a dry wind that blows in from the Sahara Desert between November and March, bringing tiny particles of sand. These form a hazy cloud or fog that can block out the sun. The sand covers everything – buildings, cars, people – with a fine film of dust. This gets into people's eyes and sometimes causes infections such as conjunctivitis. The Harmattan dust occurs mainly in northern Nigeria but has occasionally spread as far south as Lagos. It has even been known to reach the British Isles, where it is called "blood rain" and coats cars with red dust around March.

Dust carried by the Harmattan winds provides farmers near Kano with rich soil nutrients.

TEMPERATURE AND RAINFALL

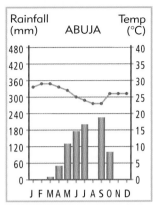

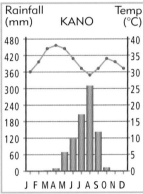

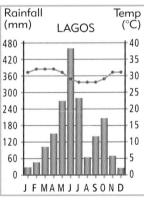

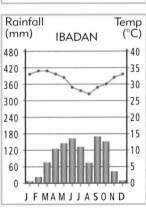

KEY:

Temperature

Rainfall

15

RIVER SYSTEMS

The rivers of Nigeria are important assets. They provide sources of energy, transport routes, food, and water for both domestic use and irrigation. The two largest rivers – the Niger and the Benue – form a *Y* shape that effectively divides the country into three. They meet almost at the center of the country. This is seen as the symbolic meeting point of the country's different ethnic and religious groups and is therefore an important site.

THE NIGER AND ITS TRIBUTARIES

The River Niger is the third-largest river in Africa and the sixth largest in the world. Of its 4,170km length, only a third lies within Nigeria, but it is still the country's longest and most important river. About two thirds of Nigeria's land is within its catchment area.

The Niger's source is in the hills of Futa Jallon in Guinea. It enters Nigeria from the west and flows in a southeasterly direction until it is joined by its major tributary, the Benue River, at Lokoja. The Benue is Nigeria's second most important river. Its source is in the hills of Cameroon and it enters Nigeria from the east.

Other important rivers in Nigeria are the Sokoto, Kyobe, Hadejia and Kaduna in the north and Ogun, Osun, Owena, Osse, Anambra and Cross River in the south.

HYDROELECTRIC POWER

The Niger and the Benue are important sources of hydroelectric power (HEP). The Kainji Dam, near Jebba, was built on the Niger in 1968 to provide power as well as water to irrigate the surrounding area. Since a series of dams was built on the Niger River and at Shiroro Gorge on the Kaduna River, hydroelectricity has provided 38 percent of Nigeria's energy needs. Power from these plants is distributed to the large towns and cities. However, many villages in Nigeria are still without any electricity at all; they burn wood as their main energy source. What is more, dam building has had serious consequences for local populations, ousting

The Niger is Nigeria's most important river, and the land around its tributaries is farmed intensively and heavily settled.

The Kainji Dam on the Niger River is Nigeria's largest dam.

farmers from their land, interrupting pastoral routes and causing severe flooding hazards (see case study).

TRANSPORT AND DREDGING

Nigeria's rivers tend to get silted up, which makes them shallow and unnavigable for large boats. In 1998, the Nigerian government decided to start dredging the Niger and the Benue from central Nigeria to the Niger Delta. The goal was to deepen the rivers and keep the water flowing, making them better equipped to ship goods and people. However, several environmental groups objected, and many riverbank communities were worried how the dredging might affect their jobs and their villages.

Particular concern has been expressed about the impact on the Niger Delta. This area already suffers from oil pollution. It is feared that the increased flow of the Niger River might speed the rate at which the river banks are eroded and lead to flooding.

Local groups protested against the dredging, particularly in the Niger Delta where they felt that only the mining companies would benefit. This held things up, but only temporarily. In 2004, after a protracted delay, the federal government commenced plans to dredge the Niger River again.

CASE STUDY
FLOODING

The damming of Nigeria's major rivers for irrigation and hydroelectricity has caused instances of serious flooding in recent years.

In 2003, heavy rains led to dangerously high water levels that threatened to burst the walls of the Shiroro Dam on the Kaduna River. Officials decided to open the gates of the dam to prevent this – but more than 100 villages downstream were flooded in the process. No lives were lost because villagers were given warnings, including radio broadcasts, before the waters were released. However, homes, schools, hospitals and fields of crops were destroyed or damaged beyond affordable repair. In other cases warnings have not been given and many lives have been lost. In October 2004, flash flooding severly damaged a church building and a home for the elderly in the southern Nigerian state of Akwa Ibom, following particularly heavy rainfall.

Small boats provide an important mode of travel in the south. Many rural roads become impassable during the rains.

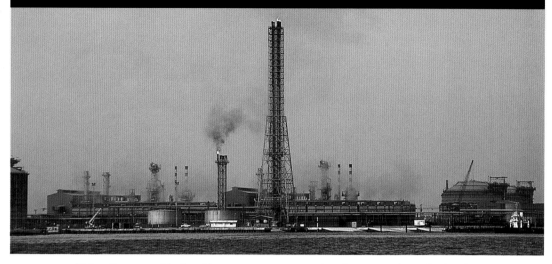

This refinery outside Port Harcourt processes crude oil into petroleum for local consumption.

Nigeria is rich in natural resources. It is the world's sixth-largest producer of crude oil and has huge reserves of minerals. It boasts plenty of fertile land that is suitable for agriculture. Its large population constitutes a skilled workforce and creates a huge market for home-produced goods.

Nigeria is potentially Africa's wealthiest country. However, this potential has yet to be realized, and very few Nigerians gain any benefit from their country's assets. Many of Nigeria's natural resources have not been exploited. This is partly because of a lack of investment – either by the government or by foreign investors – and partly because successive governments have failed to plan properly for development.

OIL – THE "BLACK GOLD"

Crude oil, sometimes known as "black gold," is by far Nigeria's most important and most exploited resource. In the late 1950s, vast reserves of crude oil were discovered in the Niger Delta region. Nigerian oil, which is known as "Bonny Light," has a low sulfur content. This makes it particularly attractive to American and European buyers since it produces less-polluting petroleum, which helps them meet the legal requirements for "clean fuel" and is easier to turn into gasoline.

REFINING OIL

There are four oil refineries in Nigeria. Three are located in the Niger Delta region and one in northern Nigeria at Kaduna. Oil is transported to the north by pipeline. By processing the oil itself – turning it from crude oil into petroleum – Nigeria can make more profit.

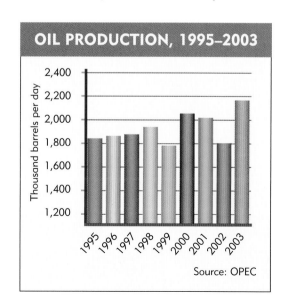

OIL PRODUCTION, 1995–2003

Thousand barrels per day (1995 to 2003)

Source: OPEC

However, the refineries often operate at only 40 percent of full capacity. They are poorly maintained and underfunded, and from time to time they have been the target of sabotage by people who object to what the oil industry is doing to their land. As a result, much of Nigeria's oil is exported and refined abroad.

FUEL SHORTAGES

Nigeria produces 90 million tons of crude oil a year, but because most of this goes to the international market, Nigeria itself sometimes suffers fuel shortages. It is therefore forced to import about 70 percent of its fuel from other countries. When Nigerians go to fill up their cars with gas, they often find that there is none or that prices are inflated because of the black market: Thousands of illegal fuel salesmen sit along the roadside selling at very high prices. Large amounts of domestic fuel disappear across the borders to Chad, Niger, Benin and Cameroon, where locals will pay up to four times as much for gasoline. This angers many Nigerians who think they should have access to cheap gas, given that their country produces so much. There have been several strikes as a result.

Surface pollution from oil platforms near Soku has caused environmental damage.

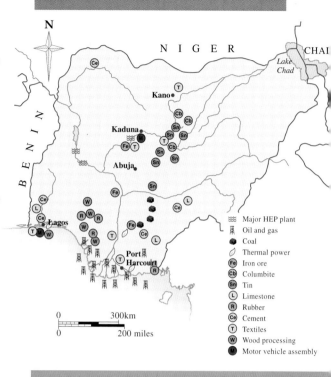

N

NIGER CHAD

Lake Chad

Kano

Kaduna

Abuja

Lagos

Port Harcourt

0   300km
0   200 miles

≋ Major HEP plant
⚒ Oil and gas
● Coal
◊ Thermal power
Fe Iron ore
Cb Columbite
Sn Tin
L Limestone
R Rubber
Ce Cement
T Textiles
W Wood processing
● Motor vehicle assembly

ENERGY DEMANDS

With Nigeria's vast and rapidly growing population, huge amounts of energy are required to meet domestic, manufacturing and business needs. In urban areas in particular, the demand for energy is increasing. More and more consumer products, such as washing machines and computers, are being used, even though the majority of Nigerians still can't afford these luxuries. Fuel resources, therefore, are a valuable commodity.

NEW RESERVES

The oil industry is expanding because of the discovery of new offshore oil fields near Akwa Ibom. These deposits are more expensive and difficult to extract, but companies are anxious to move away from the Niger Delta where they have experienced protests and demonstrations from local people over the use and pollution of their lands (see case study page 35).

ABOVE: Much of Nigeria's oil and gas is loaded onto tankers and exported for processing into other products such as fuels and chemicals.

BELOW: Tin miners near Jos. Tin mining, once a major industry on the Jos Plateau, has declined in importance since aluminum has replaced many of the uses for tin.

UNEXPLOITED MINERALS

Nigeria possesses an abundance of mineral resources other than oil. Unfortunately, most of them remain unexploited. Any kind of mining requires huge initial capital investment, and Nigeria is unable to afford this. There is some foreign investment, but many countries are still reluctant to invest in Nigeria following its recent political instability.

NATURAL GAS

Natural gas is found in abundance alongside oil in the Niger Delta. Nigeria has 5 percent of the world's estimated totals, and in 2001, annual production was about 15.7 billion m^3. Anticipating major development of this resource, a large-scale project was started in 1999 to export natural gas from Bonny Island in the Niger Delta. There are also plans to pipe gas north across the Sahara Desert to Algeria and on to Europe.

Irrigation using the traditional pulley and oxen system is still common in many parts of the north.

MINERALS AND MINING

There are sizable deposits of iron ore in the savannah region in the northern half of the country. This iron ore is generally of a low grade, but it is important for the steel industry. Nevertheless, iron ore still needs to be imported to meet demands within Nigeria. Limestone is another raw material used in the steel industry and is quarried in the valleys of the Niger, Benue and Sokoto Rivers.

Lignite (brown coal) and subbituminous coal (intermediate in quality between lignite and soft, or bituminous coal) are found and mined in southeast Nigeria. There are significant coal reserves, but the government has neglected these in favor of the oil industry. Tin and columbite are mined on the Jos Plateau, although tin mining is declining because world prices are now so low.

There are plans to exploit Nigeria's reserves of bauxite (aluminum ore) and develop its aluminum industry. Aluminum is used to manufacture lightweight products such as food cans. The problem is, as with nearly all of Nigeria's resources, that the capital investment is lacking.

WATER FOR IRRIGATION

Water is vital for irrigating agricultural land, especially in the dry regions of northern Nigeria where droughts are common. The first government irrigation projects began more than 50 years ago, and by the end of the 1960s, 9,000 hectares of land were under irrigation. There are major large-scale irrigation systems such as the South Chad Irrigation Project in Borno state and the Kano River Project, funded by the federal government in the 1970s. The money for these came mainly from the revenues from oil. Overspending on such projects has been largely responsible for the huge debt that Nigeria currently faces (see page 25).

TRADITIONAL METHODS

Many traditional irrigation methods are still used. Sometimes shallow depressions of land are created and flooded during the rainy season to conserve water. This is known as water harvesting. Particularly important for agricultural production and livestock grazing are the naturally occurring *fadamas* – seasonally waterlogged areas or stretches of flooded low-lying land. In the north, *shadoof* irrigation has been operating for hundreds of years. This device is a pivoted pole with a weight at one end and a bucket at the other, used to raise water from a well or a river. In some parts of the north, people are able to use artesian wells, which drive water to the surface from underground reserves.

Raising cattle is important in the north, but it is becoming increasingly difficult for traditional pastoralists to make a living.

FOOD FROM THE LAND

A variety of crops grow well in Nigeria's climate, and 33 million hectares of land are under cultivation. Many rural households and farms have chickens to provide eggs and keep goats and sheep for their meat. Cattle are raised on the plains of the north, but there is an increasing danger of overgrazing in these areas.

HOME PRODUCE

Most of the crops grown in Nigeria are subsistence crops – produced by farmers for their own families' use, with any surplus sold at the market. In the north, grains – such as sorghum and millet – are the staple crops. They are typically intercropped (see page 36) with cowpeas and peanuts. The wetter climate in the south is more suitable for rice, corn and yams. Cassava and tomatoes are grown throughout Nigeria.

Raising cattle is important in the north, but it is becoming increasingly difficult for traditional pastoralists to make a living.

Many subsistence farmers still use the "bucket method" to irrigate their crops.

CASE STUDY
A COCOA FARMER

Nigeria is the world's fourth-largest producer of cocoa, with 6 percent of the total supply, and cocoa is Nigeria's largest source of foreign income after oil. However, cocoa yields have been falling steadily since the 1970s, both because farmers have been reluctant to cut down their overaged trees and replace them with more productive new varieties and because the rural infrastructure is poor.

Alowonie Williams is a farmer in his mid-50s. He grows cocoa pods on his plantation near the town of Akure in the state of Ondo. Alowonie is one of 11 million people in West Africa who depend on cocoa production for their livelihood. He has seen his cocoa yields and his income fall since he started farming, and he knows that he needs to replace his old trees. But he says he can't afford to lose more income in the short term while he waits for the new trees to mature and become productive.

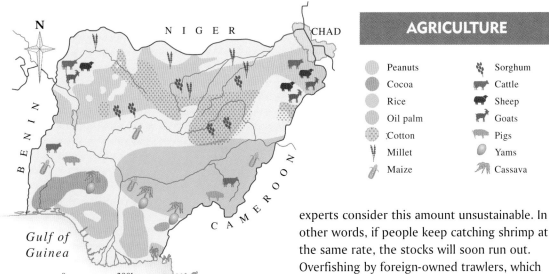

N

NIGER CHAD

BENIN

CAMEROON

Gulf of
Guinea

```
0          300km
0          200 miles
```

AGRICULTURE

- Peanuts
- Cocoa
- Rice
- Oil palm
- Cotton
- Millet
- Maize

- Sorghum
- Cattle
- Sheep
- Goats
- Pigs
- Yams
- Cassava

experts consider this amount unsustainable. In other words, if people keep catching shrimp at the same rate, the stocks will soon run out. Overfishing by foreign-owned trawlers, which fish farther out to sea, is also rapidly depleting fish stocks. Furthermore, pollution associated with the oil industry has seriously affected marine life in the Niger Delta. These factors could have disastrous results for the small coastal communities that depend on fish for their livelihoods.

The size of fish catches today may be smaller than in the past due to threatened stocks.

CROPS FOR EXPORT

Palm oil became an export crop to Europe during the nineteenth century and was used to lubricate machines in the factories and mills of England. It is now exported for the production of margarine and ice cream. Cocoa, from which chocolate is made, is another important commercial export crop – 60 percent of Nigeria's annual cocoa output comes from the so-called cocoa belt in the Ondo region.

FOOD FROM THE RIVERS, LAKES AND SEA

Fish from Nigeria's rivers and lakes and from the sea are an important source of food. Lake Chad and the Kainji Reservoir are particularly rich in fish. Dugout canoes are the traditional fishing vessels; the main difference today is that they have outboard motors. Sea fishing is based in small fishing villages all along the south coast. Boats set out to sea in search of bonga and sardinella. Fishing plays a vital role in supplying a large number of people in Nigeria with affordable, high-quality animal protein.

THREATENED STOCKS

Shrimp are fished for commercial purposes in the Gulf of Guinea, mostly for export. The catch is estimated at 4,700 tonnes a year, but

Lagos is an important industrial city and is the "economic engine" of Nigeria.

Since the 1970s, Nigeria has depended very heavily on the income it gets from oil – too heavily. Oil revenues account for 80 percent of government earnings and 90 percent of foreign exchange earnings. This means that the health of the Nigerian economy is very closely linked to world oil prices. If these fall, the country suffers.

HISTORY OF TRADE

Nigeria's economy has been closely linked to international markets in one way or another for several hundred years. Before Europeans set foot in Nigeria, there was a thriving trade in all types of commercial goods such as cotton cloth, palm oil, earthenware pots and raffia mats. These were sold across the Sahara Desert to North Africa and beyond, and in the south along the Atlantic coast.

THE SLAVE TRADE

The growth of the slave trade, between the beginning of the sixteenth century and the middle of the nineteenth century, had a devastating effect on Nigeria – and Africa as a whole – in both humanitarian and economic terms. It is estimated that Africa lost more than 20 million people to the plantations of the Caribbean and the Americas. Often the strongest and most able men and women were taken and transported across the Atlantic, leaving farms without workers.

BOOSTING THE BRITISH EMPIRE

During the nineteenth century, when British power over Nigeria increased, goods were exported to the United Kingdom. Nigeria supplied raw materials such as cotton and palm oil for the British Industrial Revolution.

OIL BOOM

Following the discovery of oil in the late 1950s, the face of the Nigerian economy changed completely. By the 1970s, with the vast revenues and income Nigeria was getting from oil, the country looked set for a very prosperous future. Many people thrived, and

The gates of the former Badagri slave encampment. Slavery had a major impact on the farming economies of Nigeria.

those in a position to take advantage of Nigeria's new status and wealth – mainly politicians and their families – made a lot of money.

The government started to invest in the country's infrastructure; it spent money on education, health care, and industrial development and on several grandiose schemes such as building new universities and roads. These increased employment, particularly in the construction industry.

OIL BUST

Confident its wealth would continue to materialize, the government took out loans from international lenders to boost its development projects. Nigeria began to import expensive Western consumer goods, such as cars, and huge sums were spent on urban improvement projects.

But in the early 1980s, oil was plentiful worldwide – in fact there was a glut – and the price fell dramatically. Nigeria had been depending almost entirely on its oil revenues, so the bubble burst. Projects had to be abandoned and the country fell into an economic depression.

Interest rates rose as fast as oil prices had dropped, and Nigeria faced huge difficulties in repaying the loans it had taken out in better days. International lenders and creditors started to call in their loans, imposing tight restrictions on the way in which the government could spend money on social programs such as education and health. These restrictions were part of what is known as a structural adjustment program.

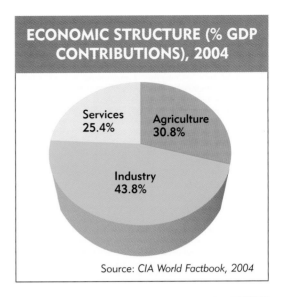

ECONOMIC STRUCTURE (% GDP CONTRIBUTIONS), 2004

Services 25.4%
Agriculture 30.8%
Industry 43.8%

Source: CIA World Factbook, 2004

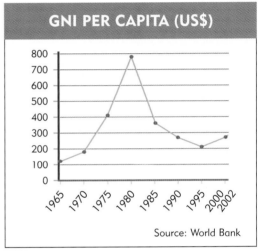

GNI PER CAPITA (US$)

Source: World Bank

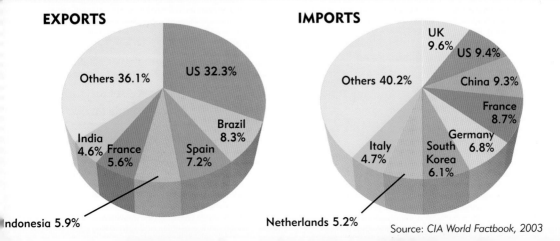

MAJOR TRADING PARTNERS (% OF VALUE), 2002

EXPORTS

Others 36.1%
US 32.3%
Brazil 8.3%
India 4.6%
France 5.6%
Spain 7.2%
Indonesia 5.9%

IMPORTS

UK 9.6%
US 9.4%
Others 40.2%
China 9.3%
France 8.7%
Germany 6.8%
Italy 4.7%
South Korea 6.1%
Netherlands 5.2%

Source: CIA World Factbook, 2003

AGRICULTURE

At the time of independence, in 1960, agriculture was still Nigeria's main source of foreign income. The Nigerian government tried to boost the domestic economy by encouraging firms to use local materials instead of relying on imports.

The oil boom had a serious effect on agriculture. In the early 1970s, when the price of crude oil was high, Nigeria could afford to import exciting new consumer goods, including agricultural produce. But these imports undermined locally produced foods and farm products, and many farmworkers flocked to the cities. During the 1980s, the government adopted a ban on the import of wheat – the staple of people in towns – in order to encourage self-sufficiency in wheat production. However, by then many farms were abandoned, and many never fully recovered. Today agriculture is still important in terms of producing food crops, and it provides employment for a large majority of the population. But Nigeria, once self-sufficient and a large exporter of food, now has to import food.

Cotton being weighed before going to market. Cotton is one of several cash crops grown in northern Nigeria.

MANUFACTURING

Nigeria's manufacturing industry is dominated by light consumer goods, such as textiles and drinks. Other products include motor-vehicle parts, pharmaceuticals and foodstuffs. However, industry is highly dependent on the import of expensive raw materials and is therefore not as profitable as it could be. Likewise, Nigeria has to pay high prices for imported machinery, which holds back development in terms of producing more goods. Manufacturing employs only about 8 percent of the workforce.

The problems exist because, in the past, a large part of Nigeria's manufacturing industry was owned by foreign companies. The Lebanese in particular have a long tradition of setting up businesses all over West Africa, especially in Nigeria. The country has attempted to change this situation so that more factories are owned and run by Nigerians using local materials.

ABOVE: Billions of dollars have been wasted on "white elephant" projects in Nigeria, such as the Ajaokuta steel plant.

CASE STUDY
REVITALIZING THE STEEL INDUSTRY?

The Ajaokuta steel plant is located in Ajaokuta in Kogi state and occupies an area of 24,000 hectares. It was originally designed in 1979 to produce 1.3 million tonnes of liquid steel per year. It was begun with Soviet funding and engineers from the Soviet Union were involved in its construction. However, in 1983 the project lost its funding and the plant fell into disrepair.

Following the restoration of democratic rule in 1999, the government – with help from the World Bank – undertook to renovate the plant. The original plant was by then very outdated and the Nigerian government had to spend more than US$5 billion to renovate and reactivate it. At the beginning of 2004, an Indian company was commissioned to continue the rehabilitation and eventually hand over the plant to the Nigerian government. However, by October 2004, the plant had closed down.

This would reduce imports, which would save money and bring more work.

Most of Nigeria's manufacturing industry is located in the south around Lagos. Attempts are being made to move production elsewhere, to avoid too much concentration in this already crowded area. Another goal is to base industry more and more on the use of local resources.

DIVERSIFICATION

Nigeria needs to look at how it can develop other industries so that the economy can become more varied. Foreign investment would help to exploit some of the country's rich resources and develop service industries such as tourism.

TOURISM

For many years, Nigeria has neglected its tourism sector. But in an attempt to bring in foreign revenue, the Nigerian government has planned and organized a new carnival in the capital, Abuja. Politicians are also looking at other cultural festivals that could be developed as part of a tourism calendar.

The government wants to create a positive cultural event to attract tourists and improve the image of Nigeria abroad. However, its notorious reputation for corruption will have to be cleaned up before any significant numbers of tourists will visit Nigeria.

The manufacture of concrete blocks near Kano is typical of the small-scale manufacturing and industrial sector found across much of Nigeria.

REASONS FOR POVERTY

It is difficult to pinpoint a single reason why Nigeria's economy is quite as poor as it is. The reasons are many, complicated and often connected to each other. But most people believe the main causes are related to corruption, government mismanagement, ethnic rivalries and an overdependence on oil. These have all led to a negative image of Nigeria abroad that has discouraged foreign investment.

CONFLICT

Since independence, Nigeria has had a succession of military governments, most of which have been toppled by a coup. Often these overthrows of the government have been violent and leaders and their followers have been assassinated. The coups have been the result of rivalries between different ethnic and religious groups, particularly the north versus the south. Against an unstable background like this, long-term planning has been impossible and Nigeria is still seen as a politically unstable country by potential overseas investors.

CORRUPTION

Government corruption became widespread during the oil boom and has continued. Political contracts were awarded to friends and family rather than being earned. Huge amounts of money went missing as military dictators deposited billions of petrodollars in Western banks. (A petrodollar is a dollar's worth of income from sales of oil to foreign countries.) This again did not inspire confidence in Nigeria abroad. Today, politicians are still being accused of spending more time debating how much to pay themselves than discussing how the country should be run.

MISPLACED PROFITS

While Nigeria does benefit from oil revenues, most of the exploration and extraction of oil is done by foreign-owned companies which take a large percentage of the profits. Nigeria does not have the capital to extract sufficient oil

High unemployment means that many people must rely on the informal economy, such as this family selling mangoes.

A worker for Shell Oil checks drilling equipment at Soku in the Niger Delta.

itself. Profits are also made from refining the oil, but Nigeria has only four inefficient refineries in place.

In effect, Nigeria has a dual economy. While there is the lucrative oil industry operating on the world stage, the vast majority of the workforce are still engaged in subsistence agriculture and are very poor. Instead of people getting richer because of oil, they have become poorer because they face lower salaries and higher prices.

OVERDEPENDENCE

Nigeria's economy is very fragile because it depends so heavily on oil. Oil accounts for almost half of Nigeria's gross domestic product (GDP) and about 90 percent of all foreign exchange earnings. Although the country is a member of the Organization of Petroleum Exporting Countries (OPEC), which sets the price for oil on the world market, it has little say in this and each price rise or fall affects Nigeria considerably.

DEBT

Underlying all of these problems, Nigeria's severe debt remains. The interest rates on its loans are so high that it seems unlikely they

will ever be repaid. Nigeria is therefore locked in a cycle of poverty. It needs money to invest in the education and welfare of its people in order to develop an effective workforce that will contribute to the economy. But dwindling oil revenues prevent this kind of spending.

CASE STUDY
SANI ABACHA

Sani Abacha was the president of Nigeria up until his death in 1998. He came to power through a military coup and was accused of abusing many human rights. He imprisoned those who opposed him, and in 1995 he had the writer Ken Saro-Wiwa executed (see page 35). Saro-Wiwa had been campaigning against the government's support for oil companies that were polluting the Niger Delta and denying the Ogoni people who lived there a share of the oil revenues. It is believed that Abacha stashed billions of dollars in foreign bank accounts. He spent the money on himself, his family and a group of his friends. Meanwhile, ordinary Nigerians were suffering great hardships. He is remembered with a sense of shame by most Nigerians.

Sani Abacha was perhaps Nigeria's most oppressive military dictator.

STANDARDS OF LIVING

Millions of ordinary Nigerians have to live with the consequences of the failing economy and the huge cuts in government spending. Over recent years they have seen their quality of life deteriorate rapidly. The vast majority of Nigerians struggle to make ends meet. Nigeria now ranks among the lowest in the world in terms of human development.

In many ways, urban Nigeria has the outward signs of a developed, modern country – there are office buildings, hospitals, universities and paved roads – but a look below the surface shows how misleading appearances can be. Much of the country's infrastructure is falling apart. Transport systems and buildings that were built in the 1970s are now falling into disrepair.

TRANSPORT

TRANSPORT – GOING NOWHERE

In the 1980s, Nigeria had one of the best-developed transportation systems in Africa, but it has failed to maintain it. Roads, dangerously full of potholes, are regularly the scenes of fatal accidents. In the 1990s, Nigeria had the highest road death rate in the world, with an average of 161 deaths for every 1,000 vehicles (the US rate was less than 1 per 1,000 vehicles). Traveling to work in cities such as Lagos and Ibadan is very difficult – as is visiting friends and family in rural villages.

Urban traffic congestion can make city travel slow and difficult.

Nigeria's railways are slow, very old-fashioned and highly inefficient. They were largely developed by the British during colonial years and have since deteriorated. Relatively cheap gasoline and the huge secondhand car market in Nigeria makes travel by car much more affordable for local people. Trains are used mainly for freight, such as distributing fertilizer during the crop-planting season.

DECLINING URBAN SERVICES

Although most Nigerians who live in towns have electricity and running water, the supplies are erratic and frequently down. Power cuts regularly plunge people into darkness and rob factories of valuable production time, leading the National Electric Power Authority (NEPA) to be dubbed "Never Ever Power Always." The power cuts often occur because of corrupt officials who skim funds from the electricity budget, and because the electricity infrastructure has been allowed to deteriorate to the point where the system can no longer cope with demand.

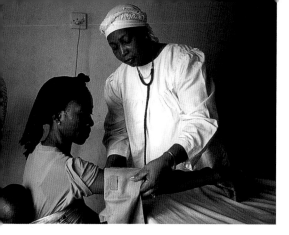

Many Nigerians do not have access to basic primary health care because it is either too expensive or unavailable.

LACK OF HEALTH CARE

The implementation of the Structural Adjustment Program in the late 1980s – the plan imposed on Nigeria so that it could pay back its debts – led to decreased spending on social programs. As a result, most Nigerians – especially those in rural areas – do not have access to basic primary health care. There is no free health service, nor are there affordable insurance plans. What is more, in many rural areas health care facilities simply do not exist. Here, people still rely on traditional medicines or simply do without. The hospitals and clinics in urban areas are available only to the wealthy.

Unofficial medicine sellers are a common sight on Nigerian streets. They offer cheap remedies, but relatively few of them have any formal medical training. Diseases caused by poor sanitation and malnutrition, as well as the high risk of HIV (see page 55), put many Nigerians in a very dangerous position.

STRUGGLING TO LEARN

Nigerians put great value on education and many receive a decent schooling. But families must struggle and make enormous sacrifices to pay for the uniforms and books their children need. It is quite common for children to have to drop out of school to work, in order to help the family survive. In rural areas, many children stay at home during peak periods of the agricultural cycle to help out on the farm. Even those who have received a good education cannot always find work. The unemployment rate among secondary school graduates is 35 to 40 percent.

SHARING THE WEALTH?

Resentment has built up among Nigerians who can see the potential for wealth that oil could bring, but who know that the vast majority of the population are missing out. The oil industry has become the target for some of their anger. Pipelines have been sabotaged and oil installations attacked by young people demanding that the oil wealth be used for everyone's benefit. It is believed that local people sometimes sabotage pipelines to create jobs for themselves, since they know that the oil companies will hire them to clean up the oil spills afterward.

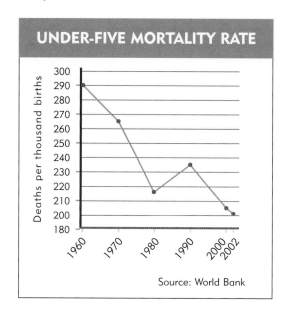

UNDER-FIVE MORTALITY RATE

Deaths per thousand births

Source: World Bank

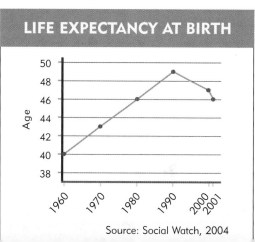

LIFE EXPECTANCY AT BIRTH

Age

Source: Social Watch, 2004

Most people in Nigeria still depend on fuelwood for household energy.

Nigeria is a country with considerable biodiversity – in other words, it has a rich range of natural environments, animals and plants. There are mangrove swamps, savannahs, rain forests, deserts and mountainous areas, with many different species of flora and fauna.

Unfortunately, Nigeria's ecology is under threat as the growing population, grinding poverty, unplanned development and climate change cause increasing damage. However, the government now recognizes that there is a problem and is taking measures to protect the environment.

THE RAIN FORESTS

Rain forests are important, wherever they are in the world, because they support many different types of animals and plants. They are often referred to as "the lungs of the world" because trees and plants return oxygen to the atmosphere. In fact, rain forests are one of the world's most precious resources. But they are

Roads through the rain forest provide commercial logging trucks with access to hardwood timber.

Exposed topsoil around Laminga is easily eroded by heavy rain.

now cover only 15 percent of the country's total land area. In the more densely populated areas, many trees have been cleared to make way for cocoa and rubber plantations. Parts of the forest have also been destroyed for road building. Clearing the land leaves the topsoil exposed to heavy rainfall and leads to erosion, making the land useless for farming of any kind.

DESERTIFICATION

Desertification is a major problem in Nigeria. Around the towns of Sokoto, Kano and Katsina in the north, much of the vegetation has been removed by continuous cropping, overgrazing and bush burning. Together with drought, this has led to desertification, the process by which an area of land becomes like a desert. First the trees disappear, leaving grasses and bushes. Finally these give way to expansive areas of desertlike sand. Some people talk about the gradual southward spread of the Sahara Desert. The situation has been worsened by massive irrigation systems, which divert water from already dry areas. Desertification is considered one of the most serious problems facing the northern states of Nigeria, which are important agricultural areas. It could have grave consequences for the whole nation.

also valued for the commercial logging of hardwood timbers such as mahogany and iroko, used for making furniture. There is a real danger that if Nigeria's rain forests continue to be felled at the rate they have been, they will soon vanish altogether.

Already between 70 and 80 percent of the original forests have disappeared, and they

CASE STUDY
FARMING IN THE NORTH

Hassan Mohamed followed in his father's footsteps and became a commercial peanut farmer in northern Nigeria. He also grew food crops for his family to eat. When he started farming, the soils were fertile and the rains reliable. At harvest time the family were able to sell some of their surplus food at the local market.

However, in the early 1980s a decade of drought began. This resulted in crop failure and the death of livestock. Large sections of

land that had been fertile were increasingly invaded by sand dunes. Hassan and his family were stricken by poverty; some of their neighbors moved to cities farther south. Hassan noticed that because many trees had been cut down, allowing water to run off the surface, the level of groundwater had dropped and the local streams and rivers were much shallower than they had been. Life has changed a lot for Hassan and his family and things are much more difficult for them today than they were 20 years ago. Hassan is no longer able to earn a living from farming and takes odd jobs whenever he can find them.

THREATS OF DEVELOPMENT

Before modern development, Nigeria's diverse habitat of mangrove swamps, tropical rain forests, savannahs and mountain plateaus supported many different species of plants and animals. However, over the last few decades, vast areas of natural habitat have been lost to land degradation, the building of towns and cities to house the rapidly growing population, industrial developments and the expansion of farmland. The homes of thousands of species of plants and animals have been destroyed.

WETLANDS AT RISK

Nigeria's rivers and lakes have fared badly under development. Wetland habitats (or *fadama* lands), which are home to many species of birds and animals, have been cleared for irrigation. Their flood-dependent ecosystems have been damaged by dam construction, which has upset the natural cycle of flooding. For example, the Jere Bowl – a previously important rice-producing area which depended on seasonal flooding – has been badly affected by a dam built in the 1980s under a multimillion dollar World Bank urban water supply project.

The largest tract of mangroves in Africa – and the third-largest in the world – lies in the Niger Delta region. Areas like this are important as fish nurseries where fish can breed. Furthermore, the mangrove plants act as buffers against erosion by waves. When the mangroves are removed, the land is easily and quickly eroded. But the delta is also under threat from oil pollution, the removal of sand for construction materials and overfishing. More than 40 percent of Nigeria's mangrove swamps have already been lost.

ENDANGERED ANIMALS

The widespread hunting of wildlife for food has increasingly threatened the animal population. Many once-common species are now found only in very remote areas or inside major reserves and game parks. These include Nigeria's few remaining elephants (which were hunted for the ivory from their tusks), buffalos, lions, leopards and other large game. Smaller animals such as antelope, monkeys, jackals and hyenas, are still found and are quite widespread. Hippopotamuses and crocodiles also remain fairly common in the largest rivers. Birds, including species that migrate seasonally between Africa and Europe, are abundant. However, some species, such as the gray parrot, are illegally exported to countries such as Saudi Arabia and could become endangered. The gray parrot is popular for its ability to mimic speech.

Leaking oil pipelines have caused large-scale environmental degradation in the fragile ecosystems of the delta.

The Ogoni people consist of about 500,000 Nigerians who live and work on or near the Niger Delta in the south of the country. They came to the attention of the world in 1995 when nine leading Ogoni campaigners, including the writer Ken Saro-Wiwa, were executed by the government. The Ogoni have long struggled against Shell Oil Company for exploiting their land. Their farming areas and fishing grounds have been polluted by oil leaks, depriving them of their livelihoods. They also suffered severe repression under the military regimes, which were determined to ensure that this major oil company did not leave Nigeria. The Movement for the Survival of Ogoni People – an organization representing their cause – campaigns for better access to oil profits.

This man is standing by what used to be a natural spring that supplied his village in Ogoniland with water. The spring was destroyed when an oil pipeline burst in the mid-1970s.

OIL AND GAS POLLUTION

Pollution from oil activities in the Niger Delta is a serious environmental problem. Some of this is by way of oil spills which contaminate the land and ruin it for farming and fishing. There have been more than 4,000 oil spills since 1960. But there is also air pollution from the burning of excess gas that comes up with the crude oil. This is known as gas flaring. It produces methane, which has more potential to create global warming than the carbon dioxide given off by cars and factories.

URBAN POLLUTION

Serious environmental problems are caused by the unplanned development of city areas in Nigeria. Lagos, for example, grew up so rapidly that there was no time, money or organization to ensure that an adequate sewerage system was in place (see page 45). Consequently, the haphazard streets crammed with makeshift homes are lined with unhealthy open sewers. The volume of cars, congested roads, and the heat, all contribute to a fog of pollution – smog – that hangs over the city on most days.

Industrial waste and plastic bags are other serious environmental hazards that many Nigerian cities share. Nigeria is a major producer of plastic bags, which are often discarded after use. Because there are no real waste disposal or recycling facilities, the bags litter the landscape. They accumulate in waterways and block drains, causing stagnant water to gather, which provides a breeding ground for diseases.

Human sewage is a common pollutant of drainage channels in the slum dwellings around Lagos.

SAVING THE ENVIRONMENT

Since Nigeria's return to democracy in 1999, there has been a renewed interest and concern for the environment by both the government and activist groups. The government, despite its lack of funds, is attempting to address some of the environmental problems the country faces. There are several active environmental groups in Nigeria putting pressure on politicians to do even more.

TRADITIONAL METHODS

There is an increased interest in traditional methods of farming, which people now realize are very effective ways of conserving the land. They have been used for centuries. One such method is intercropping, which involves planting different crops all at the same time, in the same field, to ensure an even coverage that binds the soil. Intercropping reduces erosion and also makes the soil more fertile. Another traditional method is terracing. In areas such as the Jos Plateau, where there are areas of steep land, farmers have built terraces that prevent soil creep (soil slipping downhill) and make the best use of valuable land.

Many traditional methods are very effective for preserving and using water efficiently. Earth dams, for example, are built to harvest and store water during the short rainy season in the north. The water is then used for irrigation and the reclamation of degraded farmlands.

REFORESTATION

Replanting trees helps to counteract several environmental problems. It provides habitats for animals and secures the topsoil, preventing erosion and allowing rain to soak in and replace groundwater. The government plans to increase forest cover by banning the export of timber, promoting the replanting of forests and encouraging local communities to develop their own conservation projects. In the north, acacia trees and vetiver grass are being planted to reduce erosion and slow the advance of sand dunes.

This tree nursery in Maigatari produces seedlings that are distributed to help combat desertification and provide an income.

A poster promotes forest conservation. Finding the balance between local needs and conservation is a great challenge.

The poster text reads:

Let's save

Forests link our past with the future.

NIGERIA'S REMAINING FORESTS

Our forests are disappearing fast. With their loss, we lose not only valuable timber but also many other important forest products not least being potential cures for diseases such as AIDS. If we are not careful, nothing will be left for future generations.

We need to protect our forests and replant degraded areas.

Let us practice sustainable farming.

We need to sustainably log forests and replace felled trees.

Let us all manage our precious natural resources sustainably for the benefit of future generations.

Save the Nigeria Forests Campaign is coordinated by NCF, Nigeria National Parks Service and Paignton Zoo, U.K.

Cross River state in eastern Nigeria has an exceptionally diverse and rich range of habitats and species. It is the home of several species of primates – such as gorillas, baboons and chimpanzees – migratory and resident birds, and more than 950 types of butterfly. Many of Africa's rarest trees, such as mahogany, ironwood, camwood and mimosup, are found here, but exports of these to Europe, America and Japan have been seriously depleting the forests. In the Cross River National Park, scientists do regular biodiversity surveys to monitor changes. They also consult with the Efik, Ejagham and Bekwarra peoples who live in the forest and have developed a vast knowledge of the ecology over hundreds of years. In an attempt to stop the destruction of this valuable forest area, the state's governor has suspended all logging licenses.

Baboons are one of the many protected species in Cross River National Park.

There are also a number of successful government "shelterbelt" projects in the north of the country – in Jigawa state, for example. Trees are planted in strips, or "belts," about 30m across to act as wind barriers and reduce soil erosion on the farms alongside them. Most often, it is the *neem* tree, a species imported from India, that is used because of its ability to withstand harsh environments.

NATIONAL PARKS AND RESERVES

Nigeria has a system of national parks and reserves, where the aim is to protect and conserve the natural environment and wildlife. Elephants, hippopotamuses and antelope can be seen in game reserves such as Kainji and Birnin Gwari. Gorillas, thought no longer to exist in the country, have recently been found in the dense forests of the southeast.

Nigeria cooperates with neighboring Cameroon, Chad and Niger to manage the wildlife in areas around their common borders.

POPULATION AND SETTLEMENT

Large families are common and children often serve as a valuable supply of rural labor.

Nigeria's enormous population – the largest in Africa – is one of the things for which it is most famous and earns it the nickname "the giant of Africa." In 2004 the population was estimated at over 137 million.

POPULATION GROWTH

Nigeria's population is growing rapidly – at about 3 percent per year. Some experts predict that by the year 2025, 206 million people will be living there. The population is growing so fast because there is a very high birth rate – approximately 40.16 births per 1,000 people. Each woman gives birth, on average, six times in her lifetime. The death rate is comparatively low, at 13.72 per 1,000, despite increasing fatalities due to HIV/AIDS (see page 55). Infant mortality rates are falling but are still high. It is unheard of, and considered very unlucky, to name a child before it is born because so many die during childbirth and in infancy.

FAMILY SIZE

In 1988, the government instituted the National Population Policy. This was designed to reduce population growth. It encouraged women to have fewer children and promoted the health and welfare of mothers and children to improve their quality of life. It recommended that couples should have no more than four children per family. But the policy failed. A large family is highly valued and seen as a status symbol in Nigeria. Having children is also important in a society where many infants die, and where extending the family is the best way to ensure that a person will be cared for as he or she ages. Many

POPULATION, 1950–2050

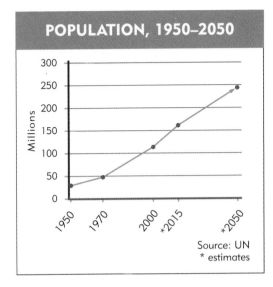

Source: UN
* estimates

farming families also prefer to have many children so that there is adequate labor to help on the farm. Nearly half of all Nigerians are younger than 15 years old. The average life expectancy is just 46 years.

POPULATION DENSITY

Nigeria's large population is not evenly distributed throughout the country. Some urban areas are very densely populated, with as many as 1,000 people per square kilometer. These include cities such as Kano and Lagos. In the rural, arid areas of the north, densities are well below 50 people per square kilometer. However, not all rural areas are sparsely populated. In parts of the countryside around Kano it is estimated that there are more than 140 people per square kilometer. Some rural areas in the south also have relatively high densities. This puts a lot of pressure on basic resources such as land for farming, water and fuelwood.

POPULATION ISSUES

Nigeria's vast population is both one of its strengths and one of its weaknesses. Various issues arise from the population's diversity and size.

ETHNIC CONFLICT

The exact size and proportion of the different ethnic groups within Nigeria has been a matter of great political controversy for many years. The number of people in each ethnic group determines how many seats they are awarded in Nigeria's House of Representatives, and therefore how much power they have in the government. In the past critics have challenged census results, claiming that they were manipulated by one or another of the different ethnic groups to show that it had a majority of the population. A census in 1973 claimed that 64 percent of the population lived in the north, but this census was rejected.

STRAINED SERVICES

Despite cuts in education funding, most Nigerians are well educated and skilled. This creates a strong labor force. Another strength is that Nigeria has a vast internal market – there are plenty of people to buy manufactured consumer products and pay for services. However, on the downside is the fact that such a vast population needs to be fed and requires certain basic social services. These are things that the government is hard-pressed to provide.

POPULATION STRUCTURE, 2004

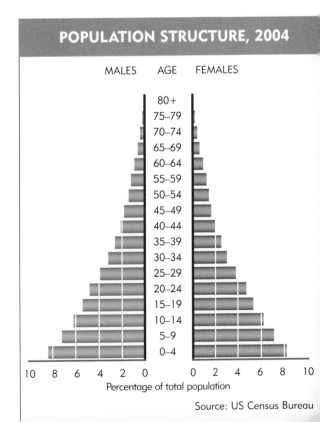

Source: US Census Bureau

URBANIZATION

Urbanization refers to the changes that take place in a country when the number of people living in cities and towns increases. In 1991, about 36 percent of Nigeria's population lived in urban areas. This has now increased to almost half the population, creating what is known as "urban bias."

People – particularly those who have had an education – leave the countryside to look for work in the cities. The factor that pulls them to the cities is the prospect of work and the expectation of a more exciting life. The factors that push them away from the countryside are

Services such as electricity, clean water and sewage disposal often do not exist in shantytowns such as this.

the scarcity of land and the poor soils, leading to declining crop yields. It is usually the young, particularly young men, who go to the cities in search of a better standard of living.

PROBLEMS AND PATTERNS

Most of the people leaving the countryside move to huge, sprawling cities in the south – Lagos, Ibadan, Warri, Benin City and Port Harcourt, for example. The northern cities of Kano, Kaduna and Sokoto are also popular. This influx of people into towns and cities has led to the rapid growth of large urban centers, creating congestion, overcrowding, poor housing, poor sanitation, unemployment, poverty and crime.

The oil boom stimulated migration to cities in the south. Since then, migration has fluctuated with the state of the economy.

Many people leave the poor soils of northern Nigeria in the hope of a better life in the cities.

URBAN POPULATION

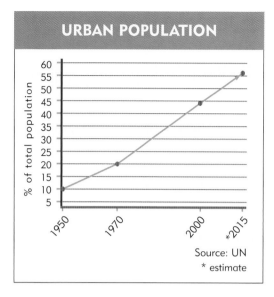

% of total population

60
55
50
45
40
35
30
25
20
15
10
5

1950   1970   2000   *2015

Source: UN
* estimate

the onset of the rains, and later return to their home villages in time to plant their own crops. The Hausa call this pattern of seasonal migration *cin rani,* which means "eating away the dry season." Even though roads are now dangerously neglected, labor shortages on some farms mean that migrant workers are willing to travel around the country working where they can.

THE BRAIN DRAIN

Nigeria is experiencing increased levels of emigration as those who have a good education – and can afford to leave – go abroad to live. Nearly every country in the world has a Nigerian community – Nigerian students and residents are found particularly in other parts of West Africa, the United States and the United Kingdom. In these communities, people continue with many of their traditional customs and festivals. Emigration is a problem for Nigeria because it loses some of its brightest and most qualified young people to other countries. However, they often send money back to their families. Throughout Nigeria this adds up to millions of dollars each year and is a key factor in helping Nigerians set up businesses.

When the economy suffers a downturn and there is a shortage of jobs in the cities, migration declines and some people return to their home villages.

SEASONAL WORKERS

The improvement in roads in the 1970s made it feasible for workers from the north to come south. They would work as hired farm laborers in the cocoa belt and elsewhere at

Nigeria must provide opportunities for its educated professionals if the "brain drain" phenomenon is to be avoided.

CASE STUDY
LEAVING FOR A BETTER LIFE

Ibrahim Olorode was born in 1967 and brought up in Ibadan in southern Nigeria. He studied accounting at a university and worked in a bank for a year. But life in Nigeria was difficult. At that time, Nigeria was still under military rule and many people did not feel free to say what they wanted. In 1996, Ibrahim left Nigeria to go to the Gambia where he worked as a teacher in a secondary school. Here he met an Englishwoman. They married and now live in England where Ibrahim is a security guard in the offices of a large insurance company in Bristol. Ibrahim says things are better now in Nigeria under civilian rule, and he would like to return to visit his family and friends one day.

ABOVE: A compound with traditional dwellings and buildings in a Hausa/Fulani village.

BELOW: Socializing is an important pastime, especially in village life.

RURAL NIGERIA

More than 50 percent of Nigeria's people still live in villages and in the countryside. Life here is almost exclusively based on subsistence agriculture, although people are increasingly taking other jobs in order to afford farm inputs such as chemical fertilizer. There have been small changes in, for example, construction materials – tin is now used instead of grass for roofing – and some mechanization of farm tools has taken place. But generally very little has altered for hundreds of years. Villages have few modern services. Women and girls usually collect water from a well or a standpipe, and more often than not there is no electricity.

EFFECTS OF URBANIZATION

Rural areas have been severely affected by mass migration to the cities. The great majority of migrants are men of working age,

Osoroko-Lekki is a Yoruba village on the Lekki Peninsula, about 70km east of Lagos. It is built in the traditional Yoruba way, with houses clustered around a communal courtyard. As brothers and sons married and brought their wives to the compound, more houses were built. If there was not enough land to build another house, a new piece of land would be found and a new line of the family established.

The village is smaller than it used to be when trade in salt with people of the northern savannah was an important economic activity. The permanent population of the village is now only about 200 people. Most of the inhabitants are mothers, children and the elderly. Others have left the village for Lagos in search of paid work, but they still regard Osoroko-Lekki as their home and return for festivals and family celebrations, showing off their city clothes.

In many ways, life in the village has changed little for hundreds of years. Some villagers still live in traditional houses made from wood and grass, all obtained locally. However, in the mid-1980s, modern concrete bungalows with piped water and electricity were built, mainly by people who returned briefly from their work in Lagos to build houses in preparation for their retirement. Around the village, slash and burn agriculture – where vegetation is cut down and burned to create fertile ash-based soil for planting – and the cultivation of new crops, such as cassava and cashew, have altered the environment.

Osoroko-Lekki is a typical Yoruba village on the Lekki Peninsula.

so the rural areas from which they come have been left with a population imbalance in favor of women, younger children and older people. Whereas, in the past, it was common for relatives to stay in the village to help raise children and care for the old people, the pressures of modern life are such that the extended family is breaking up and such ties can no longer be counted on.

As men leave the villages, jobs – such as weeding and harvesting – still have to be done, usually by women and children. Some are done by hired laborers who move around the country. However, sometimes there is no one to do the jobs at all, and farms fall into decline and become overgrown. With the growth in the population and the increased demand for food from the cities, this is a serious problem.

NIGERIA'S CITIES

Nigeria has many very large cities, all of which have certain similarities. However, cities in the north and south have developed in different ways, which are reflected in their layout and in their architecture.

CITY STRUCTURE

Precolonial Yoruba cities in the south were built as a series of compounds – enclosed areas with several buildings in which one family lived.

Some wealthy Nigerians live in modern new houses, such as this home in the suburbs of Lagos.

These compounds were part of districts, each with its own leader. Surrounding the urban area was a forest for hunting and to provide protection. Beyond this was farmland belonging to the city dwellers. Sometimes, for instance during the planting season, city men and women would stay on their farms for several days to plant or harvest. Similarly, people living

CASE STUDY
KANO

Located in the north, at the crossroads of several cultures, Kano is one of the oldest cities in sub-Saharan Africa. It dates back more than 1,000 years. Its traditional architecture reflects the influence of Islam and North Africa, with intricate, ornate patterns on walls and buildings. Kano is a classic example of a "dual city," incorporating a bustling modern center (Sabon Gari) – designed and built for those who came to live in Kano from the south – and an ancient walled Islamic city.

For centuries Kano has been one of the most active commercial centers in West Africa. Its leather goods – made from goatskin – were traded in Europe as far back as the fifteenth century. Kano was also renowned for cloth dying, and it is still possible to see people working at the famous dye-pits, coloring fabric in the same way as they have done for hundreds of years.

Kano's dye-pits date back hundreds of years and remain an interesting aspect of the city today.

Today, Kano is Nigeria's third-largest city. Cotton textiles, steel furniture, processed meats, concrete blocks, indigo dye and shoes are now manufactured here, and cotton, cattle and peanuts are traded and shipped elsewhere.

in surrounding villages often had property in the town and considered themselves town people. They divided their time between the town and the village. This close relationship between urban areas and the surrounding rural areas remains in many Yoruba cities today.

The cities in the north were historically centers of power and developed as city-states, extracting taxes from areas under their control.

THE CAPITAL CITY

Lagos used to be the capital of Nigeria, but in 1976 planners decided to move the capital to Abuja. This new city was built in the center of the country in an effort to end the ethnic troubles of the past by favoring neither north nor south. Abuja was built on land independent of any ethnic or religious group, and its central location was to be a symbol of greater cooperation between all Nigerians. It officially became Nigeria's capital in 1991 and is the base of the central government. In 2004 it hosted peace talks for another African country, Sudan, meant to resolve its Darfur crisis (a bloody conflict between the Arab government and rebel black African groups in western Sudan).

CASE STUDY
LAGOS

Lagos, on Lagos Island, was established in the fifteenth century. It began as a trading post between the Kingdom of Benin and Portuguese traders, exporting ivory, peppers and slaves. When Nigeria fell into the hands of the British, they began exporting food crops.

The heart of Lagos is the area known as Eko. This is where the commercial and administrative headquarters of the city are. It is linked to the mainland by three bridges and to Okoyi and Victoria Islands by road. These are the residential areas where richer Nigerians live.

But most of the city is the result of rapid, haphazard building that started in the early 1970s, when thousands of people moved here from the countryside. At the same time, refugees and migrants

Lagos epitomizes many of the problems that many large African cities face, including crime, unemployment, pollution and urban sprawl.

from other African countries arrived. It is now a chaotic, dirty city that consumes 45 percent of Nigeria's energy. Much of the housing is substandard and the sewerage system is inadequate. Traffic is extremely heavy: It can take two to three hours to travel 15km across the city. The crime rate in Lagos is particularly high, with carjackings, burglaries, and e-mail and Internet scams high on the list of offenses. Rich Lagos residents – who may have something to steal – live in high-security communities equipped with electric fencing and patrolled by armed guards.

Christian church services, such as this one in Lagos, are important community social events.

With more than 250 different ethnic groups, Nigeria is a complex cultural mix. It reflects both African and Islamic traditions, as well as Western influences – though more recently and to a lesser extent.

RELIGION

Nigeria's main religions are Islam and Christianity. Some people follow traditional religions, such as animism – the belief that natural objects such as trees and rocks are inhabited by powerful spirits – and often these beliefs are incorporated into the main religions.

A mosque in Abuja. The city was built on land independent of any religious group, and now Christians and Muslims there live side by side.

In the north, the Hausa and Fulani people are mainly Muslim and make up about half the population. This means that Nigeria has one of the largest communities of Muslims in the world. The Yoruba and Igbo in the south, making up 40 percent of the population, are mainly Christian, although some are Muslim.

Unfortunately religion is one of the major factors that divides Nigerians. It has been the cause of serious outbreaks of violence in recent years. In 2000 some northern states

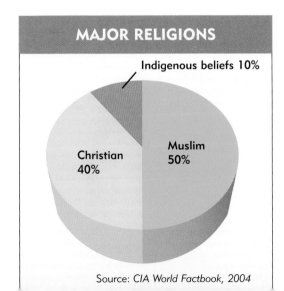

MAJOR RELIGIONS

Indigenous beliefs 10%

Christian 40%

Muslim 50%

Source: CIA World Factbook, 2004

This classroom in Ibadan illustrates the poor conditions and overcrowding that are typical of most Nigerian schools.

introduced Islamic law, or Sharia, to reinforce the Islamic way of life – largely as a response to Westernization. Sharia makes certain activities – such as adultery – criminal offenses, and strict punishment is applied. Many non-Muslims who live in these states object to Sharia law, creating much conflict.

LANGUAGE

It is estimated that more than 500 different languages are spoken in Nigeria. Some of these are understood by only a few hundred people. On the islands of the Niger Delta, there are villages only a few kilometers apart where people speak completely different languages – so different that they are incomprehensible to each other.

Children in schools are taught in English, which is also used in government, business and the media, although nearly everyone speaks their own language at home. Nigerians think nothing of being able to speak three or more languages. A simplified form of English, or pidgin English, is widely spoken in the south of the country, similar to the pidgin spoken in Liberia and Sierra Leone, where it is called Krio.

EDUCATION

Education, particularly Western-style education, is seen as a way of gaining a better job and income and greater status in society. In rural areas, children learn skills from their family or on the job as a kind of apprentice, either in addition to or instead of going to school.

Levels of education are highest in the south. This is generally thought to be due to Western-style teaching, which was introduced to Nigeria by (and associated with) Christian missionaries. In the north, many Muslim people are still suspicious of Western education, because they feel that there is a hidden agenda to dilute the Islamic religion. Thus many traditional families in the north choose to send their children to Muslim Koranic (or Qur'anic) schools, where they are taught in Arabic.

FAMILY LIFE

In Nigeria, as in many other African countries, the family unit is still relatively strong and a powerful sense of community exists. Extended families – where several generations of a family live together – are common, especially in rural areas. Older people are particularly well respected. Nigerians are often shocked when they hear that people in Western countries allow their elderly parents to live in nursing homes, rather than taking care of them themselves. However, things are changing now and the pressures of modern life sometimes have the effect of loosening the ties binding the extended family.

CASE STUDY
THE ORAL TRADITION

In Nigeria, as in other parts of Africa, people developed a way of passing on their history by word of mouth. Much of the history of a family or ethnic group is learned through stories or poems that explain the history of their ancestors. These are then passed down and added to through the generations. In northern Nigeria, due to the frequent droughts, the subject of much Hausa oral history is about feast and famine. Talking drums – held under the arm and played with a stick – are a traditional form of communication in rural areas. They are used as an imitation of speech, to convey messages from one village to another, and to recite history and sing praises to the chief.

Weddings are major financial responsibilities, and families must plan for them years in advance.

LITERATURE AND COMMUNICATION

Nigerians are avid newspaper readers and radio listeners. They like to know what is going on in the world and enjoy debating and arguing about topical issues. There are many different daily newspapers, most in English but some in local languages such as Yoruba and Hausa.

Many Nigerian writers have gained world recognition for their novels and poems. Chinua Achebe wrote about the effects of colonial rule on traditional ways of life. Wole Soyinka has written poetry, plays, novels and nonfiction and was awarded the Nobel Prize in literature in 1986.

CELEBRATIONS AND FESTIVALS

In Nigeria there is always an excuse to have a party, and both Christian and Muslim festivals are celebrated to the full. Christmas Day, Good Friday, and Easter Monday – as well as Eid-al-Fitr (the end of Ramadan), Eid-al-Kabir and Eid-al-Maulud – are all national holidays.

The Islamic festivals in northern Nigeria are spectacular occasions when brightly dressed men on decorated horses take part in processions, followed by wrestlers and musicians.

Boat races and fishing festivals also take place. The famous Argungu festival in Sokoto is a very popular attraction. Hundreds of fishermen dive into the river and emerge a short while later with fish they have caught in their bare hands. Many festivals are related to the harvesting of crops, such as the Yam Festival in the southeast.

Weddings and naming ceremonies are lively events often attended by hundreds of people. The music, dancing and feasting can last for several days. Even funerals are cause for celebration: Many people believe that death means joining the ancestors, so the deceased must be given a good sendoff. However, these ceremonies are often major financial obligations and Nigerians must plan years in advance to pay for them.

ART

Islamic influences are to be seen in the arts, especially in the architecture of the north. However, Islam does not allow the representation of people or animals in art forms, so ceremonial carvings are virtually absent in Muslim states. The national Museum in Lagos has a rich collection of art from all periods. The Nigerian government has sought to prevent the removal of significant Nigerian art from the country and to return art taken abroad during the colonial era.

CRAFTS

Wood carving is the most common form of artistic expression, especially among those who live in the south. Ebony (which is black) and white wood are most often used. The ancestral and ceremonial wood carvings of the Benin, Igbo, Ibibio and Yoruba artisans are among the most beautiful works of art.

Traditional textiles include embroidery, weaving, *adire* (tie-dye) and silk-screen printing. *Adire* is traditionally associated with the people of Abeokuta, Ibadan and Osogbo, but modern designs using *adire* are found elsewhere in Nigeria. Leatherwork, metalwork, glass beadwork, raffia and grass weaving, and calabash carving (a calabash is a type of gourd) are popular in different parts of the country.

Drumming is a popular pastime and also an important part of Nigerian culture.

MUSIC

Music is the driving force of any occasion or event in Nigeria. It is central to the way Nigerians celebrate and express themselves. Songs and dances are played on drums, flutes, trumpets, stringed instruments, xylophones and thumb pianos. Music is an integral part of receptions, marriages, naming ceremonies and even job promotions.

Traditional and modern music are both widespread. Pop music can be heard in the nightclubs of the cities and towns and on the radio. "Highlife" and "Juju" bands mix Western music with African beats and instruments. Famous Highlife artists are King Sunny Ade and Ebenezer Obe. Lagos is the most important city for modern music in West Africa, and musicians come from all over Africa to perform here.

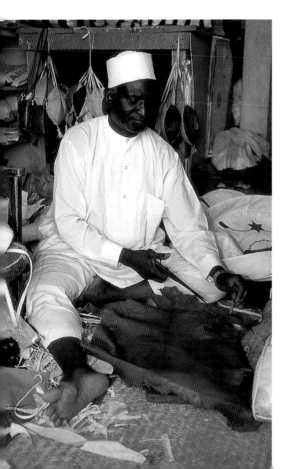

This leather craftsman in Zaria continues to work using centuries-old traditional methods.

FOOD

Traditional Nigerian food is based on local produce such as vegetables, meat and fish. It is cooked into stews and soups and eaten with rice, cassava or yams. But in the cities fast food, such as burgers, and food from street vendors, such as deep-fried beancakes, are increasingly popular. Bread has become the main urban staple.

A widely eaten dish is boiled yams, which are pounded to make something similar to mashed potatoes. This is called *fu-fu* and is eaten with a vegetable, meat or fish stew. Rice is commonly cooked with ground tomatoes, peppers and meat or fish. Palm oil is a thick, rich, reddish-brown oil made from ground palm kernels and is often used in cooking. Some Nigerian food is cooked in hot chili sauce. In the north, *tuwo* is the staple food, made from rice or the flour of millet or sorghum. It is cooked in boiling water and stirred until thick, then served with a spicy sauce or soup.

MEALTIMES

At mealtimes, people gather round one bowl and eat with their hands or a spoon. Even soup may be eaten with the hand. Men usually dine separately from women and children. Hospitality is at the heart of the Nigerian lifestyle, so visitors are always invited to share a meal.

Fast food has become increasingly popular in Nigeria, although many take-out restaurants still serve traditional dishes.

LEISURE

Nigeria has a long tradition of theater. Plays are often based on biblical stories, comedies, political satires and protests. Movies are increasingly popular, and Nigeria has its own film industry, known as "Nollywood," producing films that are distributed all over West Africa.

On the weekends people enjoy going to watch a wrestling match, or they play *ayoby yor,* a traditional board game using seeds or stones. Marbles, skipping, clapping and singing games and flying kites are all popular with children. Wealthy Nigerians living in the urban areas often belong to sports clubs and gyms, but these are inaccessible to most people.

SPORTS

Sports are hugely popular in Nigeria. Just about every sport imaginable is played in Nigeria, including basketball and baseball, golf and tennis – but football (soccer) is the most popular by far. The national team is called the Super Eagles and several members also play for UK and European clubs, where salaries are high. Nigeria's team won the gold medal in the 1996 Olympics in Atlanta, and in 2002 they qualified for the World Cup finals. Nigeria also has a national women's soccer team that has

Soccer is the most widely followed sport in Nigeria, and it is one of the country's great passions.

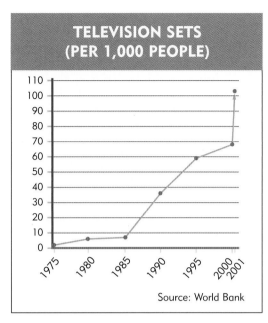

TELEVISION SETS (PER 1,000 PEOPLE)

Source: World Bank

participated in the Olympic Games. Several Nigerians have moved to the United States and Canada to play professionally in sports such as basketball and boxing.

Running is another sport at which Nigerians excel and where they have achieved success at international level – particularly the 100m and 200m sprint events. Wrestling is a traditional Yoruban sport which has a big following.

MOBILE PHONES

The growth in the use of mobile phones in Africa as a whole and in Nigeria in particular has been phenomenal. The old fixed landline system was so poor that people have welcomed mobile phones with open arms. For most Nigerians, a cell phone is the first phone they have ever owned, owing to the huge expense and poor availability of landline phones.

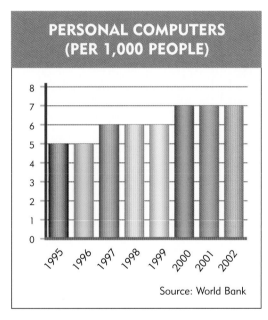

PERSONAL COMPUTERS (PER 1,000 PEOPLE)

Source: World Bank

TELECOMMUNICATIONS DATA (PER 1,000 PEOPLE)

Mainline Phones	6
Mobile Phones	13
Internet Users	3

Source: World Bank, 2002

Nigerians are great talkers and mobile phones allow them to stay in touch with their family and friends. They have become the most important means of communication. The average time that a person uses a mobile phone in a week in Nigeria is 200 minutes, compared with 120 in Britain and 143 in the United States. Mobile phones are often shared among several people. Some people set up businesses on street corners, offering their phones to customers willing to pay by the minute to make a call.

Collecting water from wells is one of the many tasks that women must undertake.

WOMEN IN NIGERIA

Nigerian women have always played an important role in the family and in society. They are expected to be the wage earners in the family, and they do most of the farming, as well as fishing, herding and trade. Women are also the mainstays of family and cultural life, and they are playing an increasing role in business and politics.

WOMEN AT WORK

Women do up to 80 percent of the farming in Nigeria and produce two-thirds of the food crops. This is in addition to their household chores of fetching water, cooking and looking after children. They often spend up to 16 hours a day working.

In every town in Nigeria there is a market. Women go there to buy food and to sell any surplus produce they may have. They are also places where women can meet each other and catch up with the latest gossip. They are colorful, lively and noisy places, with much chattering and bargaining going on.

In order to make extra money, women do jobs such as hairdressing, soap making or mat weaving. Groups of women often form cooperatives to help each other profit. For instance, some women's groups set up savings systems whereby they all put in a certain amount of money each week and take turns borrowing the money. This enables them to pay for expensive items, such as a sewing machine or some chickens, or to set up a small business.

Women are responsible for much of the household and farm work. These women near Kano are weeding their sorghum plot.

WOMEN AND ISLAM

In the north, where most people are Muslims, men are allowed to have more than one wife. In homes without modern conveniences, this can make life easier for women because they can share the chores. The custom of keeping women separate from the rest of society and covered with head-to-toe clothing, known as purdah, prevents women from taking part in many social and political activities.

Islamic law, or Sharia (see page 47), has brought in new rules and punishments, many of which affect women more than men. One Islamic court ruled that a woman found guilty of adultery should be stoned to death, but there was an international outcry and the decision was reversed. Separate schools for girls and single-sex taxis are other features of this gender discrimination.

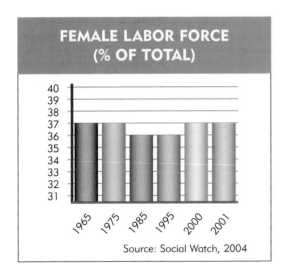

These girls are wearing *hijabs*, part of the traditional Islamic dress.

WOMEN AND CHILDREN

Given the option, the majority of Nigerian women would choose to have fewer children. They are among the most likely women in the world to die because of complications during pregnancy. Midwives, town criers and village health providers are involved in education about family planning, and the use of contraception among married women 15 to 49 years old has increased from 3 to 15 percent in some parts of Nigeria.

If a family is short of money, it is likely that girls will be forced to leave school rather than boys. In an attempt to redress this, schools are opening especially for women who have missed out on education.

FEMALE LABOR FORCE (% OF TOTAL)

40	
39	
38	
37	
36	
35	
34	
33	
32	
31	

1965 1975 1985 1995 2000 2001

Source: Social Watch, 2004

CASE STUDY
THE MISS WORLD CONTROVERSY

In 2002, the Miss World beauty contest was to be held in Abuja, the capital of Nigeria. Many Muslims were unhappy about this because they believed that parading women in this way was immoral and against their religion. When a Nigerian journalist wrote a newspaper article claiming that the prophet Muhammad would have approved, thousands took to the streets of the northern city of Kaduna in protest. They burned churches and looted shops, and more than 100 people were killed. The contest was hurriedly moved to London. Meanwhile, the journalist involved (herself a woman) became the subject of a *fatwa* – a religious order calling for her death – by the government of Zamfara state. She was forced into hiding.

Inequality is a major problem in Nigeria. This businessman is wealthy, but most of the population remains poor.

Nigeria stands at a crossroads. A famous Nigerian author, Chinua Achebe, once claimed that Nigeria was one of the most disorderly nations in the world. It certainly faces huge challenges, but the potential to develop into a thriving, productive and wealthy nation still remains. Certain hurdles have to be overcome, however, before that can happen.

TACKLING POVERTY

Poverty is still a growing problem in Nigeria despite the estimated US$280 billion earned from oil since the 1970s. According to the World Bank, about 66 percent of the population now live below the poverty line, compared with 43 percent in 1985. The reality of this is that prices of basic goods are rising dramatically, and the incidence of malnutrition is increasing, particularly among children. This situation is particularly bad in the extreme northeast and northwest, where significant numbers of children suffer from rickets and are undernourished. Growing poverty and the huge gap between the rich and the poor are a source of unrest. Finding a solution is therefore an important challenge for the government.

In an attempt to reduce poverty, Nigeria has adopted the UN Millennium Development Goal of reducing by half the proportion of people whose income is less than US$1 a day. They also aim, between 1990 and 2015, to halve the proportion of people who suffer hunger.

Urban environmental problems, such as those visible here at the edge of Kano, are becoming increasingly common.

DEMOCRACY AND THE ECONOMY

First and foremost, the considerable wealth gained from the oil industry needs to be used so that it benefits all Nigerians more equally, and not just a few. The government must create jobs, provide good health and education services and ensure that it is free from corruption. Nigerians need to be able to trust their country's leaders.

For the last 30 years Nigeria has been poorly served by a succession of bad governments. A more stable, democratic and less corrupt government will attract investment from abroad, enabling the country to diversify and exploit more of its valuable resources. This will not only benefit the country in terms of revenues, but will reduce its dependence on oil as its only major resource.

Nigerians would like the international community to recognize that it will be impossible for Nigeria to ever pay back its foreign debts and to write them off.

The government needs to make HIV/AIDS awareness campaigns a top priority if the spread of the disease is to be halted.

THE AIDS THREAT

Nigeria is one of five countries in the world identified as being most at risk from the HIV/AIDS virus in the future. In the past, the government has not given it the priority it deserves because of political instability and a lack of political will.

There has been a huge increase in the number of HIV/AIDS cases in the last 15 years, though the problem has not been as severe as it has been in southern Africa. However, it would be dangerous for the government to ignore it because the rate of increase in cases is escalating. It is thought that by 2004 about 2.3 million Nigerians had died from AIDS, while another 3.8 million were HIV-positive. But statistics are unreliable because the stigma of AIDS often makes people reluctant to come forward for treatment.

The government has set up an HIV/AIDS Emergency Action Plan to look at ways it can tackle the problem in the short term. However, there are few medical resources available to people infected with the virus, and most people cannot afford the many drugs that are required to fight it.

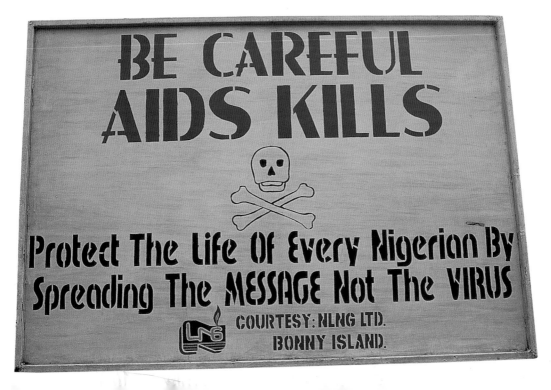

Many beautiful beaches along the south coast offer great potential for tourism development.

NIGERIA'S REPUTATION ABROAD

Nigeria is notorious for stories of violence, crime, bribery and corruption. Even teachers have been accused of accepting bribes to give students high marks in examinations. Obviously there is truth in this, yet it would be misleading to draw conclusions solely from these claims. The vast majority of Nigerians are honest and hardworking people, and things are already improving since the ending of military rule.

Improving Nigeria's reputation is important to attract not only foreign investment in industries and resources, but also overseas tourists. With its beautiful landscapes and rich heritage, Nigeria has the potential to be a vibrant and fascinating tourist destination, bringing in much-needed foreign currency. Nigeria is of particular interest to the descendants of black Africans (known as the African Diaspora) who live abroad – mainly in the United States – and are interested in their personal history and heritage. But the dangers of traveling to Nigeria

are frightening away many potential tourists. To gain their confidence, the country would have to develop costly infrastructure, such as safe and efficient transportation and lodging. However, many Nigerians might suggest that their own basic needs should come first.

ONE NATION?

Nigeria is a country of 137 million people, 500 languages and 36 states – but it is a single nation. Frequent outbreaks of violence between different ethnic and religious groups have led some people to question whether this nation can ever be harmonious. The federation of 36 states was set up in an attempt to address the diversity of Nigeria's population and to allow different areas a degree of self-government. But many people feel the current structure is unworkable because it has led to a huge bureaucracy of governors, deputy governors, permanent secretaries, advisers and more. In some cases, 90 percent of the state's income goes to pay the wages of these people.

A proposal that the 36 states be merged into six larger and more powerful states is being considered. Another proposal is that

Nigeria be split into at least two completely separate countries – an Islamic and Hausa/Fulani north and a basically Christian and Yoruba/Igbo south. This would, of course, be problematic because all the oil wealth would remain in the south. There are also those who believe passionately that Nigeria should remain as one nation.

THE FUTURE

Nigeria's greatest asset continues to be its people. They are energetic and resourceful and face the problems of everyday life with stoicism and humor. Nevertheless, some are prepared to stand up against the corruption they see around them, and there are many strikes and demonstrations against what they consider to be injustices. Several Nigerians have been imprisoned in the past for their stand against the abuse of human rights in Nigeria.

When Nigerians look to the future they face many challenges. After years of military rule, they hope for a more peaceful and stable future and for the opportunity to benefit from their country's wealth. Nigeria continues to have the potential to become a powerful, industrialized nation – with the right leadership. Democracy

One of the many new government buildings in Abuja, Nigeria's rapidly expanding capital.

should bring the public freedom of speech, access to information and the opportunity to stamp out corruption and growing inequality.

With continuing conflict in the Middle East, Western countries are likely to become more interested in Nigerian oil to reduce their dependency on current suppliers such as Iraq and Saudi Arabia. This could strengthen Nigeria's position on the world stage.

Nigeria's young people will soon have the country in their own hands. They are hopeful for a brighter future.

AIDS (Acquired Immune Deficiency Syndrome) An illness in which the body's protective system breaks down.

Air mass A large body of air with common characteristics.

Animism The belief that all natural forces and objects, living and nonliving, have souls.

Arid A term used to describe an environment with an annual rainfall that is below 250–300mm.

Artesian well A well that is drilled through impermeable rock into water-saturated rock. Pressure forces the water to flow upward.

Biodiversity The variation (diversity) of biological life within an area.

Capital investment Money needed to start up or develop businesses and industry.

Catchment area The geographical area from which streams and tributaries drain into a river, lake or sea.

Colonial Describing a system in which one country is occupied and ruled by another foreign country.

Commodity An item that can be bought and sold.

Conjunctivitis An infection that causes inflammation of the eye.

Coup d'etat A sudden and decisive takeover of government by a small group, illegally and/or by force.

Crude oil Oil in the form in which it is extracted, before it has been refined.

Delta A low area where a river divides before entering a larger body of water, usually a sea or an ocean.

Diversification The process of increasing the variety of industries and businesses in a country's economy.

Dredging The process of removing of material from the bottom of a river or estuary.

Ecosystem A system that represents the relationships within a community of living things (plants and animals) and between this community and its nonliving surroundings. An ecosystem can be as small as a pond or as large as the Earth.

Equatorial The conditions that exist in the area around the equator. In climatic terms this usually means hot and wet.

Erosion The way in which the Earth's surface is worn away by the action of water and wind.

Ethnic group People of the same race or nationality who share a distinctive cultural identity.

Federation A country that is divided into regions (states) whose individual governments take charge of much of their own affairs, leaving a lesser role for the central government.

GDP (Gross Domestic Product) The monetary value of goods and services produced by a country in a single year.

Glut A situation in which there is so much of a particular product that the price falls.

GNI (Gross National Income) The monetary value of goods and services produced by a country plus any earnings from overseas in a single year. It used to be called Gross National Product (GNP).

Habitat The environment in which any living organism lives.

HEP (hydroelectric power) Electricity generated by water as it passes through turbines.

Humidity Wetness in the atmosphere.

HIV (Human Immunodeficiency Virus) An infection that leads to AIDS.

Infrastructure The basic foundation of a country that includes the roads and railways, bridges, buildings, communication networks and waste-disposal systems.

Irrigation The controlled addition of water to dry agricultural land in order to improve plant growth.

Islam The religion of Muslims. Muslims believe that there is one God and that Muhammad was the last prophet.

Malnutrition The physical state of having eaten too little food or food without enough nutrients.

Mangroves A tropical tree or bush that grows on the edge of saltwater. It has prop roots that bind to mud, reducing erosion.

Muslim A believer or follower of Islam.

Plantation An area of land where cash crops are grown on a large scale.

Plateau An area of relatively high, flat land.

Rain forest Dense tropical forest with high rainfall.

Ramadan The ninth month of the Islamic calendar when Muslims fast during the day.

Reservoir A lake used to store water. Some reservoirs are artificial.

Rickets A childhood disease caused by a lack of Vitamin D.

Sabotage A deliberate act of destruction in which equipment and machinery is damaged to disrupt work.

Savannah A flat grassland area in tropical or subtropical areas.

Sedimentary rocks Rock that is formed from the accumulation of organic or physical matter.

Subsistence farming Farming that provides for the basic needs of the farmer, with little left over to sell.

Sustainable Something that is capable of lasting and carrying on in the long term.

Tributary A stream or river that flows into a larger river.

Undulating Describes a landscape with gently rolling hills.

Urbanization The process of people moving from the countryside to towns and cities.

Volcanic plug The resistant rock at the center of a volcano that remains when the rest of the volcano has been eroded.

Watershed A line that divides two adjacent river basins.

Yam A starchy root crop, comparable to the sweet potato. It can be baked or boiled and mashed.

FURTHER INFORMATION

BOOKS TO READ:

Achebe, Chinua. *Things Fall Apart*. New York: Anchor Books, 1994. A classic novel depicting Nigerian tribal life before and after the coming of colonialism, first published in 1958.

Bowden, Rob, and Roy Maconachie. *The Changing Face of Nigeria*. Chicago: Raintree, 2004. Illustrated reference for ages 9–12 presenting the people, resources, government, and economy of present-day Nigeria.

Giles, Bridget. *Nations of the World: Nigeria*. Chicago: Raintree, 2004. An illustrated study of the land, people, and history of Nigeria and its position in the world today.

Saro-Wiwa, Ken. *A Forest of Flowers*. Port Harcourt, Nigeria: Saros, 1986. A collection of 19 short stories of daily life and human nature in Africa, some set in a remote village and others in the city.

Saro-Wiwa, Ken. *A Month and a Day: A Detention Diary*. New York: Penguin Books, 1995. An account by the writer and environmentalist of his detention by the Nigerian government.

WEBSITES:

The CIA World Factbook
http://www.cia.gov/cia/publications/factbook/geos/ni.html
The US Central Intelligence Agency's online guide, with statistics and assessments of all countries of the world.

allAfrica.com
http://allafrica.com/nigeria/
Articles and news about Nigeria.

Lonely Planet
http://www.lonelyplanet.com/destinations/africa/nigeria/
General information about Nigeria aimed at travelers.

METRIC CONVERSION TABLE

To convert	to	do this
mm (millimeters)	inches	divide by 25.4
cm (centimeters)	inches	divide by 2.54
m (meters)	feet	multiply by 3.281
m (meters)	yards	multiply by 1.094
km (kilometers)	yards	multiply by 1094
km (kilometers)	miles	divide by 1.6093
kilometers per hour	miles per hour	divide by 1.6093
cm^2 (square centimeters)	square inches	divide by 6.452
m^2 (square meters)	square feet	multiply by 10.76
m^2 (square meters)	square yards	multiply by 1.196
km^2 (square kilometers)	square miles	divide by 2.59
km^2 (square kilometers)	acres	multiply by 247.1
hectares	acres	multiply by 2.471
cm^3 (cubic centimeters)	cubic inches	multiply by 16.387
m^3 (cubic meters)	cubic yards	multiply by 1.308
l (liters)	pints	multiply by 2.113
l (liters)	gallons	divide by 3.785
g (grams)	ounces	divide by 28.329
kg (kilograms)	pounds	multiply by 2.205
metric tonnes	short tons	multiply by 1.1023
metric tonnes	long tons	multiply by 0.9842
BTUs (British thermal units)	kWh (kilowatt-hours)	divide by 3,415.3
watts	horsepower	multiply by 0.001341
kWh (kilowatt-hours)	horsepower-hours	multiply by 1.341
MW (megawatts)	horsepower	multiply by 1,341
gigawatts per hour	horsepower per hour	multiply by 1,341,000
°C (degrees Celsius)	°F (degrees Fahrenheit)	multiply by 1.8 then add 32

African dress is often very colorful and is an important part of Nigerian culture.

A traffic interchange in Kano, the largest city in northern Nigeria.